THE WIT AND WISDOM OF

Don Quixote

DE LA MANCHA

Edited and with an Introduction

by

Harry Sieber

McGraw·Hill

New York   Chicago   San Francisco   Lisbon   London   Madrid   Mexico City
Milan   New Delhi   San Juan   Seoul   Singapore   Sydney   Toronto

Library of Congress Cataloging-in-Publication Data

Cervantes Saavedra, Miguel de, 1547–1616.
    The wit and wisdom of Don Quixote de la Mancha / by Miguel de Cervantes
    Saavedra ; as translated by Tobias Smollett ; edited and with an introduction by
    Harry Sieber, with Holly McGuire.
    Cervantes Saavedra, Miguel de, 1547–1616.
        p.   cm.
    Includes index.
    ISBN 0-07-145095-5
    1. Cervantes Saavedra, Miguel de, 1547–1616—Quotations.
   2. Cervantes Saavedra, Miguel de, 1547–1616—Translations into English.
  I. Smollett, Tobias George, 1721–1771.   II. Sieber, Harry Charles.
  III. Title.

   PQ6329.A5T4   2004
863′.3—dc22   2004060991

1 2 3 4 5 6 7 8 9 0   FGR/FGR   0 9 8 7 6 5

ISBN 0-07-145095-5

A few paragraphs of the Introduction have been adapted or taken from a published
lecture by Harry Sieber, "Don Quixote and the Art of Reading" (Waco, Texas, 1998)
and from "Don Quixote de la Mancha: A Digital Exhibit" (http://quixote.mse.jhu.edu).

McGraw-Hill books are available at special quantity discounts to use as premiums
and sales promotions, or for use in corporate training programs. For more
information, please write to the Director of Special Sales, Professional Publishing,
McGraw-Hill, Two Penn Plaza, New York, NY 10121-2298. Or contact your local
bookstore.

This book is printed on acid-free paper.

Contents

Contents

Contents

INTRODUCTION

Miguel de Cervantes Saavedra, Spain's greatest literary figure, came of age as advances in information technology and the expansion of educational opportunities transformed Western Europe. Previously, reading had been the privilege of a small, educated elite, those with sufficient wealth or influence to acquire literacy skills and manuscripts. The world of words changed rapidly after the invention of the printing press in the fifteenth century. Europeans now possessed a relatively inexpensive means to reproduce books and circulate them in multiple copies. Spanish university towns had presses by the 1480s. A century later there were printers in most major cities and towns, producing a variety of texts for an expanding audience.

Literacy rates rose because of a parallel revolution in education. Spain had only six universities in 1470, yet there were thirty-two by the time Cervantes published *Don Quixote de la Mancha*. In the second half of the sixteenth century, Jesuits founded grammar schools in most large Spanish population centers, and many smaller municipalities hired schoolmasters to establish primary and secondary schools. Spaniards in ever-increasing numbers learned to read while Cervantes was pondering his career choices. What they chose to read was another matter.

Readers demanded news and entertainment. Spain was the leading superpower of the sixteenth century, challenging other emerging nation-states in Europe and waging sporadic war against the Ottoman Turks in the Mediterranean. While Spanish armies conquered the Americas, Spanish fleets explored previously unknown oceans. Printed broadsheets allowed the public to read the latest news from the battlefront.

Those who read for pleasure preferred adventure stories with a martial twist. Romances of chivalry, recounting the exploits of valiant knights and their ladies, dominated the Spanish fiction market in the half-century before the birth of Cervantes. Their warrior-heroes, whose origins were often shrouded in mystery, traversed alien landscapes defending the helpless and combating evil. They battled giants and rescued damsels, sometimes using magic weapons and the aid of enchanters. These knights vanquished successive challengers, decapitating and dismembering their foes. The texts described superhuman exploits in graphic and gory detail.

Moralists decried the content of chivalric romances. Books populated by giants, dwarfs, and overendowed men and women and accounts of the supernatural, magic, and enchantment seemed dangerous. Critics asserted that the secret births and adulterous relationships described were morally reprehensible and that the reading of such material was more than a waste of valuable time. They suggested that such works might be addictive, stimulating a desire to read other dangerous books. Readers would inevitably neglect their moral and social responsibilities. Despite the warnings, romances of chivalry had widespread appeal, feeding a seemingly insatiable appetite for imaginative fiction. Publishing became a lucrative industry as printers sought new copy to occupy their workshops, booksellers searched for new products to peddle, and readers demanded new entertainments.

Miguel de Cervantes entered this changing world in 1547, born in Alcalá de Henares, a university town near Madrid, where he was baptized on October 9 in the parish church of Santa María. We know little about his early life. He was the fourth of seven children, born to an itinerant surgeon who struggled to maintain his practice and his family by traveling the length and breadth of Spain. Cervantes received some early formal education in the school of the Spanish humanist Juan López de Hoyos, who was teaching in Madrid in the 1560s. His first literary efforts, poems written to commemorate the death of the Spanish queen, date from this period. Despite these early publications, nothing in the years that followed suggested that the young man would become Spain's most respected writer.

Cervantes suffered from both bad luck and bad timing. As a twenty-one-year-old student, he wounded another man in a duel. When a warrant was issued for his arrest in 1569, Cervantes fled to Seville, then to Rome, where he served in the household of an Italian nobleman. He joined the Spanish army a year later. At the Battle of Lepanto in 1571, he received serious wounds and lost the use of his left hand. After a lengthy recovery and further military service, he departed Italy for Spain in 1575, only to be captured by Barbary pirates during the return journey. He was taken to Algiers and imprisoned for five years, until Trinitarian friars paid a considerable sum for his ransom. This experience would leave an indelible mark on his later work, which contains numerous references to the themes of freedom and captivity. The disabled veteran returned to Spain deeply in debt for the ransom paid to gain his release. In 1584, Cervantes applied for a government position in the New World but was turned down. At the age of thirty-seven, he married a woman almost twenty years his junior and obtained employment as a government agent in southern Spain, requisitioning wheat and olive oil for the Invincible Armada (1588). Within two years of the defeat of the Armada, he again requested permission to emigrate to the Americas, but his petition was rejected and he was told to find some gainful employment "at home."

Thus Cervantes, already known as a promising author, began his career as a writer. In 1585, he had published his first work in prose, the *Galatea*, a pastoral romance that attracted qualified praise from some of his contemporaries. He began writing for the theater and composing short stories, some of which were later included in his *Exemplary Tales*. His most famous work, *Don Quixote de la Mancha*, was published in two parts in Madrid. Part One appeared in 1605 and the second part in 1615. The novel was an immediate success. The first part went through six editions in the year of its publication and was soon translated into English and French. The fame of *Don Quixote* brought Cervantes to the attention of a wide audience. After 1605, his work was in demand. His collection of short stories appeared in Madrid in 1613; his satiric poem *Journey to Parnassus* was published a year later; and in 1615, Cervantes was able to publish some theatrical works that had never been presented on stage. His final prose fiction, *The Travails of Persiles and Sigismunda*, whose dedication he finished four days before he died, was assessed by Cervantes as among the best of his work, competing even with the writings of the legendary Greek author Heliodorus.

Despite his national and international reputation, his death, probably on April 22, 1616, seems to have gone virtually unnoticed by his contemporaries. Cervantes was buried on April 23, 1616, in a Trinitarian monastery a few blocks from his Madrid home, but the specific location of his tomb is unknown.

Don Quixote de la Mancha

Cervantes's masterpiece narrates the adventures of an aging gentleman driven mad by misreading popular fiction. Alonso Quijano believes that the tales of chivalry in the books he reads are literally true. Quijano reinvents himself as the knight-errant Don Quixote and abandons his home to search for adventure on the highways and in the rural landscape of imperial Spain. Like the gallant knights he has read about, Don Quixote hopes to right all manner of wrongs and to gain fame for his valorous deeds. To serve as his squire, Don Quixote selects his neighbor Sancho Panza, an illiterate but shrewd peasant primarily interested in eating and drinking. Don Quixote sets forth to impose the code of chivalry on all those he encounters. Sancho follows him in search of prosperity, believing Quixote's promise that after faithful service he will be rewarded with an island kingdom that he alone will rule. The two prove to be most incompatible travel companions. Don Quixote views the world through a fog of literary illusion; Sancho Panza sees only material reality. When the knight and his squire observe clouds of dust on the horizon, Don Quixote perceives two armies at war, while Sancho correctly identifies them as passing flocks of sheep. When Don Quixote is convinced that the windmills he encounters are giants, Sancho rightly insists that they are only windmills. In the conflict between art and nature, nature often gains the upper hand.

Part One of the novel takes Don Quixote from his small village in la Mancha to the forests of the Sierra Morena, then returns him to the village to recuperate from multiple injuries inflicted at the hands of real and imagined enemies. Don Quixote meets a variety of characters on his journey, peasants and noblemen, criminals and priests, prostitutes and insane lovers, wronged women and jealous men. Cervantes uses the encounters to satirize the society in which they all exist and to comment on the codes of behavior reflected in their actions and life stories. Characters exchange views on love, both courtly and conjugal, and on chivalry, particularly the comical chivalry practiced by Don Quixote.

The second part of the novel, composed after the success of Part One and published ten years later, is more complex. Don Quixote and Sancho meet characters who have read the first part of the novel and thus already know about the pair's previous adventures. Instead of confronting what each perceives to be "reality," as they did earlier in the novel, Don Quixote and Sancho participate in adventures that are staged by and created for the benefit and amusement of the other characters. The Baroque metaphor of the world as a theatrical stage, familiar to all readers of Elizabethan drama, literally becomes true within the world of the novel. The consequences of this shift are profound. Role-playing and insanity become confused. Both Don Quixote and Sancho inhabit a world created by human artifice and imagination. Don Quixote gradually regains his senses in Part Two, driven to sanity by the eccentric, and sometimes demented, behavior of the characters he has encountered.

The early readers of Cervantes's masterpiece, in Spain and beyond, enjoyed Don Quixote as farce, almost a comic book character. He journeys through their seventeenth-century world, proclaiming the ideals of medieval knighthood. His squire is a practical peasant, more concerned with personal biology than with chivalry. The absurd misadventures of this unlikely pair are the stuff of slapstick comedy. Cervantes clearly intended to evoke laughter, often at the expense of his protagonists, but the author also uses the hyperliterate knight and his illiterate sidekick to explore the more serious relationship between literature and experience. Cervantes exploits the comedic consequences of madness, but his underlying focus is an investigation of the impact and influence that books exert on the behavior of readers, both within and beyond his text. Like Don Quixote, many of the characters who inhabit the world of the novel are avid readers. The author is more interested in *how* his characters read than in *what* they read.

The novel is about the complex relationship between reading and experience. For Cervantes, imaginative literature, condemned by moralists and church authorities alike, is the vehicle through which he can address the idea of reading and explore how readers comprehend reality and construct meaning by applying different reading strategies. Don Quixote loves to read fiction. And that, Cervantes tells us, is fine. There is nothing wrong with getting lost in a good book. Don Quixote gets into trouble when he begins to interpret events in the world around him as extensions of the fiction he has read. That, Cervantes warns us, is madness. Those who choose this reading strategy lose their identity.

Proverbs and Wit

Many of the observations in *Don Quixote* are expressed through proverbs, generally understood to be brief and witty sayings that reflect folk wisdom. Cervantes defined proverbs as "short sentences dictated by long and sage experience" (Smollett I, iv, 12; DQ I, 39). "Every proverb is strictly true; all of them are apothegms dictated by experience herself" (I, iii,7; DQ I, 21). Their topics are as varied as human experience itself: love, marriage, fear, superstition, religion, good, evil, fate, life and death, honor, justice, governance, courtesy, liberality, opportunity, hope, nobility, happiness, and truth. Their origin can be classical or biblical as in the *Aphorisms* of Hippocrates or the *Book of Proverbs*. Others are popular in nature, drawn from oral tradition. Whether they are called proverbs, apothegms, aphorisms, maxims, or adages, they convey insights into and assessments of human behavior to readers and listeners. Cervantes warns against their inappropriate use: "a proverb, unseasonably introduced, is rather an absurdity than a judicious apothegm" (II, iv, 15; DQ I, 67). In *Don Quixote*, most proverbs are placed in the mouth of Sancho Panza, who is accused of "bring[ing] them in by the head and shoulders so preposterously that they look more like the ravings of distraction than a connected chain of conversation" (II, iii, 11; DQ II, 43). Sancho's remarks, however, often go to the heart of the matter under discussion and reflect the wide division between folk wisdom and the erudition of literary culture.

Readers enjoyed the nuggets of wit and wisdom with which authors larded their writings. The sixteenth and seventeenth centuries witnessed great interest in the collection and publication of proverbs. Some scholars compiled proverbs, together with their classical origins, and published them as erudite encyclopedias. Others were content to explain the meaning of proverbs, elucidating their historical and cultural contexts. English novelist and translator Tobias Smollett (1721–1771) acknowledges the problematic links between language and context in the introduction to his version of *Don Quixote*, noting that as translator he "has endeavored to retain the spirit and ideas, without servilely adhering to the literal expression, of the original; from which, however, he has not so far deviated as to destroy that formality of idiom, so peculiar to the Spaniards, and so essential to the character of the work" (I, Preface). In cases where translation is virtually impossible, he adds explanatory notes to enlighten his readers. In other cases, he turns Cervantes's prose into witty sayings that do not appear as proverbs in the original text.

The Translator's Art

The book you are reading is based on the Tobias Smollett translation, which first appeared in 1755. His eighteenth-century idiom does in fact capture some of the "peculiar" flavor of the Spanish original, but the dated vocabulary and style are not always readily understood by modern readers. In this volume, the editors have adhered closely to Smollett's language but have at times added a word or two [placed in brackets], rearranged word order, and edited punctuation when necessary to clarify meaning. We have not included all the proverbs in Smollett's translation or in Cervantes's novel. Our purpose is to compile a representative selection organized by themes and topics to celebrate the four-hundredth anniversary of the publication of the first part of *Don Quixote* (1605). References appear at the end of citations for those who wish to locate the proverbs in their original contexts in both Smollett and Cervantes. Smollett divided his translation into volumes, books, and chapters (I, i, 3); Cervantes organized the original Spanish text into parts and chapters (DQ I, 3).

The language of the proverbs and sayings is Smollett's, but the wit and wisdom belong to Miguel de Cervantes.

Translation from one language to another, as Cervantes cautions us near the end of *Don Quixote*, "is like the wrong side of a Flemish tapestry, in which though we distinguish the figures, they are confused and obscured by ends and threads, without the smoothness and expression which the other side exhibits; and to translate from easy languages argues neither genius nor elocution, nor any merit superior to that of transcribing from one paper to another" (II, iv, 10; DQ II, 62). Smollett clearly did more than transcribe the novel from one language to another. One wonders what Cervantes would have thought had he seen his masterpiece clad in an English mantle.

—HARRY SIEBER

Our Players

Don Quixote de la Mancha: Knight of the Rueful Countenance and Knight of the Lions

A country gentleman ... who bordered upon fifty, was of a rough constitution, extremely meager and hard-featured, an early riser ... and addicted to reading of books of chivalry.

I, i, 1; DQ I, 1

He is a tall, meager, long-legged, [lantern]–jawed, stalking figure; his hair inclining to gray; his nose hooked and aquiline, with long, straight black mustachios.

II, i, 14; DQ II, 14

[His] tall stature ... [the] sepulchral meagerness of his aspect, his solemn gravity, the strangeness of his armor, all together [formed] such a composition as perhaps had never been seen in that country.

II, i, 16; DQ II, 16

The redresser of grievances, the righter of wrongs, the protector of damsels, the terror of giants, and [the] thunderbolt of war.

I, iv, 25; DQ I, 52

The most agreeable madman who ever lived!

II, iv, 13; DQ II, 55

Sancho Panza

A peasant in the neighborhood [of Don Quixote], a
very honest fellow, if a poor man may deserve that
title, but one who had a very small quantity of brains
in his skull.   I, i, 7; DQ I, 7

A person of a short stature, swag belly, and long
spindleshanks.   I, ii, 1; DQ I, 9

[Sancho's] equipage, matted beard, corpulency, and
diminutive stature ... furnished food for admiration to
everybody.   II, iii, 13; DQ II, 45

[Sancho] exposed his posteriors, which were none of
the smallest.   I, iii, 6; DQ I, 20

Sancho Panza is one of the most pleasant squires that
ever served a knight-errant: sometimes his simplicity is
so arch that to consider whether he is more fool or
wag yields abundance of pleasure; he has roguery
enough to pass for a knave and absurdities sufficient to
confirm him a fool; he doubts everything and believes
everything; and often, when I think he is going to

3

discharge nonsense, he will utter apothegms that will raise him to the skies: in a word, I would not exchange him for any other squire. II, ii, 15; DQ II, 32

Dulcinea del Toboso

[Don Quixote] avows as mistress of his heart one Dulcinea del Toboso, formerly known by the name of Aldonza Lorenzo. II, i, 14; DQ II, 14

Dulcinea . . . is the queen and lady of my soul; her beauty, supernatural, in that it justifies all those impossible and chimerical attributes of excellence which the poets bestow on their nymphs; her hair is of gold, her forehead the Elysian Fields, her eyebrows heavenly arches, her eyes themselves suns, her cheeks roses, her lips of coral, her teeth of pearl, her neck alabaster, her breast marble, her hands ivory, her skin whiter than snow, and those parts which decency conceals from human view are such, according to my belief and apprehension, as discretion ought to enhance above all comparison. I, ii, 5; DQ I, 13

Don Quixote attacks wine skins in the
belief that they are giants' heads.
Adolphe Lalauze (1838–1906)

My lady Dulcinea is enough to stupefy the five senses.

II, i, 10; DQ II, 10

Was it not enough, ye knaves, to change the pearls of my lady's eyes into a couple of cork-tree galls and her hair of shining gold into the bristles of a red cow's tail; and in short to transmography every feature of her countenance without your meddling with the sweetness of her breath by which we might have discovered what was concealed beneath that bark of homeliness?

II, i, 10; DQ II, 10

This same Dulcinea so often mentioned . . . is said to have had the best hand at salting pork of any woman in la Mancha.

I, ii, 1; DQ I, 9

Adversity

Adversity having lasted so long, prosperity must be now at hand.   I, iii, 4; DQ I, 18

Once the tide of misfortune heaped up by one's malignant stars begins to descend with violence and fury, [then] no earthly mound can oppose nor human industry divert its course.   I, iii, 13; DQ I, 27

Out of the frying pan into the fire.   I, iii, 4; DQ I, 18

One mischance invites another, and the end of one misfortune is often the beginning of a worse [one].
                                                                    I, iv, 1; DQ I, 28

He who lives much time will bear much misfortune.
                                                                    II, ii, 15; DQ II, 32

Arms and the Man

The affairs of war are more than anything subject to change.

I, i, 8; DQ I, 8

The circumstances of war . . . cannot be accomplished without sweat, anxiety, and fatigue.

I, ii, 5; DQ I, 13

Though the toil of a soldier is greater [than that of a scholar], his reward is much less.

I, iv, 11; DQ I, 38

The soldier who executes his captain's command is no less valuable than the captain who gave the order.

I, ii, 5; DQ I, 13

A covetous soldier is a monster which is rarely seen.

I, iv, 12; DQ I, 39

A soldier who falls in battle makes a much more noble appearance than he who saves himself by flight.

II, Prologue

The Knight of the Mirrors jousts with Don Quixote.

Adolphe Lalauze (1838–1906)

The wounds that appear in a soldier's countenance and bosom are so many stars to guide the rest of mankind to the heaven of honor.   II, Prologue

The good soldier acquires reputation in proportion to the obedience he pays to his captain.   II, ii, 7; DQ II, 24

The fewer enemies the better.   II, i, 14; DQ II, 14

In war, activity and dispatch anticipate the designs of the enemy and obtain the victory.   I, iv, 19; DQ I, 46

There are times for attacking; there are also seasons for retreating.   II, i, 4; DQ II, 4

It is far [easier] to reward two thousand scholars than thirty thousand soldiers.   I, iv, 11; DQ I, 38

The victor [is] always honored in proportion to the fame of his vanquished foe.   II, i, 14; DQ II, 14

Beauty

All sorts of beauty do not equally affect the spectator; some, for example, delight the eye without captivating the heart.

I, ii, 5; DQ I, 13

It is well known that the beauty of some women hath its days and seasons and is diminished or increased according to the circumstances that happen.

I, iv, 14; DQ I, 41

Beauty alone attracts the inclinations of those who behold it.

II, ii, 5; DQ II, 22

Tears of afflicted beauty soften rocks to cotton and transform tigers into gentle lambs.

II, iii, 3; DQ II, 35

Beauty in a virtuous woman is like a distant flame—and a sharp sword afar off—which prove fatal to none but those who approach too near them.

I, ii, 5; DQ I, 14

Character

*Don Quixote bullies a barber into giving him his basin, which
Don Quixote believes to be "Mambrino's Helmet."*

Adolphe Lalauze (1838–1906)

Self-commendation is in effect self-dispraise.

I, iii, 2; DQ I, 16

One man is no more than another, unless he can do more than another.

I, iii, 4; DQ I, 18

Everyone [is] the son of his own works.

I, iv, 20; DQ I, 47

Tell me your company, and I will tell you your manners.

II, i, 10; DQ II, 10

Which is the greatest fool: he who is made so by nature, or he who makes himself one?

II, i, 15; DQ II, 15

Value yourself more upon being a virtuous man of low degree than upon being a proud man of noble birth.

II, iii, 10; DQ II, 42

Blood is hereditary, but virtue is acquired.

II, iii, 10; DQ II, 42

Courage

Difficulties are undertaken either for the sake of God [or] of this world or both.   I, iv, 6; DQ I, 33

Valor lies in the middle between the extremes of cowardice and rashness.   II, i, 4; DQ II, 4

A stout heart flings misfortune.   II, i, 10; DQ II, 10

A cat that is confined, provoked, and persecuted turns into a lion.   II, i, 14; DQ II, 14

It favors more of rashness than of true valor for one man to attack a whole army in which death and emperors fight in person.   II, i, 11; DQ II, 11

When a brave man flies, he must have discovered some odds or foul play.   II, ii, 11; DQ II, 28

The achievements of a rash person ought to be ascribed rather to good fortune than courage.

II, ii, 11; DQ II, 28

Death and Dread

We are all mortal: here today and gone tomorrow.

II, i, 7; DQ II, 7

No man in this world can promise himself more hours
of life than God is pleased to grant him.

II, i, 7; DQ II, 7

Death is deaf, and when he knocks on the door of life
is always in a hurry and will not be detained either by
fair means or force, by scepters or miters.

II, i, 7; DQ II, 7

There is a remedy for everything but death.

II, i, 10; DQ II, 10

There is no trusting to Mrs. Ghostly—I mean
Death—who gobbles up the gosling as well as the
goose . . . and tramples down the lofty turrets of the
prince as well as the lowly cottage of the swain. That
same lady [Death], who is more powerful than coy,
knows not what it is to be dainty and squeamish, but
eats of everything and crams her wallet [satchel] with
people of all nations, degrees, and conditions: she is

21

none of your laborers that take their afternoon's nap,
but mows at all hours, cutting down the dry stubble as
well as the green grass; nor does she seem to chew, but
rather swallows and devours everything that falls in
her way; for she is gnawed by a dog's hunger that is
never satisfied; and though she has no belly, plainly
shews herself dropsical and so thirsty as to drink up
the lives of all the people upon earth, just as one
would swallow a draught of cool water.

II, ii, 3; DQ II, 20

We must all die and there is an end to the whole.

II, ii, 7; DQ II, 24

The life of man alone runs lightly to its end . . .
without hope of renewal, except in another life, which
knows no bounds.

II, iv, 1; DQ II, 53

The dead to the bier, and the living to good cheer.

I, iii, 5; DQ I, 19

The cat to the rat, the rat to the rope, the rope to the
gallows.

I, iii, 2; DQ I, 16

The more you stir it the more it will stink.

I, iii, 6; DQ I, 20

Genius is always attended by evil fortune.

I, iii, 8; DQ I, 22

Fear hath many eyes.

I, iii, 6; DQ I, 20

How unexpected are the accidents which at every turn befall those who live in this miserable world.

II, iv, 3; DQ II, 55

A man goes to bed well at night, but cannot bestir himself next morning.

II, ii, 2; DQ II, 19

Don Quixote in victory.

Adolphe Lalauze (1838–1906)

The Devil

He that seeks evil, may he meet with the devil.

I, iii, 6; DQ I, 20

The devil is not often found napping. I, iii, 1; DQ I, 15

The devil is very cunning and raises blocks under our feet over which we stumble and very often fall.

I, iii, 9; DQ I, 23

The devil, when he would seduce those who are on their guard, transforms himself from an imp of darkness into an angel of light. I, iv, 6; DQ I, 33

Every fiend may stink of brimstone. I, iv, 4; DQ I, 31

The devil skulks behind the cross. II, iii, 1; DQ II, 33

Diligence

Diligence is the mother of success.   I, iv, 19; DQ I, 46

That which is easily got is little valued.   I, iv, 7; DQ I, 34

The assiduity of the solicitor hath brought a very
doubtful suit to a very fortunate issue.   I, iv, 19; DQ I, 46

Works that are trumped up in haste are never finished
with that perfection they require.   II, i, 4; DQ II, 4

We eat our bread with the sweat of our brows—
which is one of the curses that God denounced
against our first parents!   II, i, 13; DQ II, 13

We cannot catch trouts without wetting our clouts
[trousers].   II, iv, 19; DQ II, 71

Though the load must lie over the ass, he must not be
overloaded.   II, iv, 19; DQ II, 71

From him who can knead and bake, it is not easy to
steal a cake.   II, iii, 1; DQ II, 33

We must fervently pray and hammer away.
                                                 II, iii, 3; DQ II, 35

Laziness . . . never saw the accomplishment of a good
wish.   II, iii, 11; DQ II, 43

The abbot must not want who for his bread doth
chant.   II, iv, 8; DQ II, 60

Etiquette and Decorum

When thou are at Rome, follow the fashion of Rome.

II, iv, 2; DQ II, 54

Nothing is so reasonable and cheap as good manners.

II, iii, 4; DQ II, 36

Garb ought always to be suited to the dignity and function of the profession.

II, iii, 10; DQ II, 42

A slovenly dress denotes a disorderly mind.

II, iii, 11; DQ II, 43

Abstain from eating garlic and onions lest your breath should discover your rusticity.

II, iii, 11; DQ II, 43

All affectation is disagreeable.

II, iii, 11; DQ II, 43

Those persons who cannot receive are not capable of giving an affront.

II, ii, 15; DQ II, 32

The courtly Don Quixote meets a judge and his lady.

Adolphe Lalauze (1838–1906)

Experience

The longer we live, the more we learn.   II, ii, 15; DQ II, 32

It is not all gold that glitters.   II, iii, 1; DQ II, 33

A saint may sometimes suffer for a sinner.

I, i, 7; DQ I, 7

One swallow makes not make a spring.   I, ii, 5; DQ I, 13

Till you hedge [put barriers, like hedges] in the sky,
the starlings will fly.   I, iii, 11; DQ I, 25

A bird in hand is worth two in the bush.   I, iv, 4; DQ I, 31

If the blind lead the blind, they are both in danger of
falling into the ditch.   II, i, 13; DQ II, 13

One ought not to talk of halters in the house of a man
who was hanged.   I, iii, 11; DQ I, 25

There are more tricks in town than you dream of.

I, iv, 19; DQ I, 46

Nobody knows the heart of his neighbor.

II, i, 14; DQ II, 14

Every season has its reason.   II, iv, 3; DQ II, 55

All seasons are not the same.   II, iii, 3; DQ II, 35

Where you meet with no hooks, you need expect no
bacon. [Bacon was normally displayed on hooks.]

II, i, 10; DQ II, 10

Fame, Honor,
and Reputation

The desire of fame is a most active principle in the
human breast.   II, i, 8; DQ II, 8

One of the things ... which ought to afford the
greatest satisfaction to a virtuous and eminent man
is to live and see himself celebrated in different
languages and his actions recorded in print with
universal approbation.   II, i, 3; DQ II, 3

If I rob you of honor, I rob you of life; since a man
without honor is worse than dead.   I, iv, 6; DQ I, 33

Honor and virtue are the ornaments of the soul,
without which the body, though never so handsome,
ought to seem ugly.   I, ii, 5; DQ I, 14

Honor may be enjoyed by a poor, but never by a
vicious, man.   II, Prologue

Small be his grace who counts himself base.
                                           I, iii, 7; DQ I, 21

Sancho Panza discovers Don Quixote's defeat by the windmills.

Adolphe Lalauze (1838–1906)

Nobody will remember what he was but [instead will] reference what he now is.   II, i, 5; DQ II, 5

Praise is always the reward of virtue and never fails to attend the righteous.   II, i, 6; DQ II, 6

There is a great deal of valor and reputation to be acquired in war.   I, iv, 12; DQ I, 39

A good name is better than tuns [large casks] of wealth.   II, iii, 1; DQ II, 33

Fortune

Every man is the maker of his own fortune.

II, iv, 14; DQ II, 66

Providence may turn the scale, and what is lost today may be retrieved tomorrow. I, i, 7; DQ I, 7

There is nothing certain in this life. I, iii, 1; DQ I, 15

Destiny, when one door is shut, always leaves another open. I, iii, 1; DQ I, 15

Fortune never ceases to persecute the virtuous.

I, iii, 2; DQ I, 16

It is impossible that either good or bad fortune should be eternal. I, iii, 4; DQ I, 18

Every man must fall by his own fortune. I, iii, 12; DQ I, 30

Good fortune seldom comes pure and single.

I, iv, 14; DQ I, 41

Fortune turns faster than a millwheel, and those who were yesterday at top may find themselves at bottom today.

I, iv, 20; DQ I, 47

When the heifer is offered, be ready with the rope; and when good fortune comes to thy door, be sure to bid it welcome.

II, i, 4; DQ II, 4

He that's coy when fortune's kind may after seek but never find.

II, i, 5; DQ II, 5

Take advantage of the favorable gale that blows.

II, i, 5; DQ II, 5

[Can] any man brag of having put a spoke in fortune's wheel? No one, to be sure.

II, ii, 2; DQ II, 19

Friendship and Generosity

Among friends, we ought not to stand upon trifles.

I, iv, 3; DQ I, 30

Suspicion should never find harbor with true and virtuous friendship.

I, iv, 6; DQ I, 33

When your neighbor's son comes to the door, wipe his nose and take him in.

II, i, 5; DQ II, 5

Good men ... may try and avail themselves of their friends ... but not presume upon their friendship in things contrary to the decrees of heaven.

I, iv, 6; DQ I, 33

The man who has a large heart is endowed with more valor than he whose heart is of smaller dimensions.

II, ii, 6; DQ II, 23

He who gives freely, gives twice.

I, iv, 7; DQ I, 34

A generous gift the rock will rift.

II, iii, 3; DQ II, 35

Our heroes find themselves on an "enchanted bark."

Adolphe Lalauze (1838–1906)

God and Faith

God shines upon the good and the bad, and sendeth
rain to the wicked as well as to the righteous.

I, iii, 4; DQ I, 18

It is the attribute of God alone to know times and
seasons: to him there is neither past nor future, but all
things are ever present to his eyes.   II, ii, 8; DQ II, 25

God, who provides all things, will not be wanting to
us.   I, iii, 4; DQ I, 18

Not a leaf can move upon a tree without the
permission of God.   II, i, 3; DQ II, 3

God is the understander of all things.   II, i, 5; DQ II, 5

When God sends the morning, the light shines upon
all.   II, iii, 17; DQ II, 48

Heaven never fails to favor the righteous design.

I, iv, 7; DQ I, 34

Heaven usually assists the righteous intent of the simple while it confounds the wicked aims of the cunning.   I, iv, 33; DQ I, 50

Various are the paths by which God conducts the good to heaven.   II, i, 8; DQ II, 8

God will order things better, for he inflicts the wound and will also perform the cure.   II, ii, 2; DQ II, 19

God will better our condition if we deserve his mercy.
                                                  II, i, 5; DQ II, 5

God's blessing is better than early rising.   II, iii, 2; DQ II, 34

There is a God in heaven who will take care to chastise the wicked and reward the righteous.
                                                  I, iii, 8; DQ I, 22

One man must not depend upon another but trust in God alone.   II, i, 4; DQ II, 4

*Sancho Panza believes that a duchess has
granted him governorship of an island.*

Adolphe Lalauze (1838–1906)

It is not part of a good Christian to revenge the
wrongs he hath suffered.   II, i, 11; DQ II, 11

He is a good preacher who is a good liver.
                                            II, ii, 3; DQ II, 20

Be thou a father to the virtuous and a stepfather to
the wicked.   II, iii, 19; DQ II, 51

Man projects in vain, for God doth still ordain.
                                            II, iv, 3; DQ II, 55

Governance and Justice

Nothing is so delicious as to command and be
obeyed.   II, iii, 10; DQ II, 42

All laws fall within the province of letters and learned
men.   I, iv, 11; DQ I, 38

Great posts and offices of state are no other than a
profound gulf of confusion.   II, iii, 10; DQ II, 42

The intent of all well-governed commonwealths—in
permitting plays to be acted—is to entertain the
common people with some honest recreation in order
to divert those bad humors which idleness usually
engenders.   I, iv, 20; DQ I, 20

When the head aches, all the members are affected.
                                            II, i, 2; DQ II, 2

It must be a very pleasant thing to govern, even tho' it
should be but a flock of sheep!   II, iii, 10; DQ II, 42

How will [a man] be able to govern other people who cannot govern himself?   II, iii, 1; DQ II, 33

Every governor must have a beginning in the art and mystery of government.   II, iii, 1; DQ II, 33

Governors, tho' otherwise fools, are sometimes directed in their decisions by the hand of God.

II, iii, 13; DQ II, 45

Great talents and learning are not necessary in a governor.   II, ii, 15; DQ II, 32

All governors are not descended from the kingly race.

II, iii, 10; DQ II, 42

Let no man meddle with a governor or his substitute.

II, iii, 11; DQ II, 43

A good governor will stay at home, as if he has a broken bone.   II, iii, 2; DQ II, 34

A covetous governor will do very ungoverned justice.

II, iii, 4; DQ II, 36

Might overcomes right.

II, iii, 11; DQ II, 43

It is not seemly that honest men should be
executioners of their fellow creatures on account of
matters with which they have no concern.

I, iii, 8; DQ I, 22

Severity is not more respected than compassion in the
character of a judge.

II, iii, 10; DQ II, 42

If you ever suffer the rod of justice to be bent a little,
let it not be warped by the weight of corruption but
the bowels of mercy.

II, iii, 10; DQ II, 42

In another man's cause, be not blinded by private
affection.

II, iii, 10; DQ II, 42

Abuse not him in word whom you are resolved to
chastise in deed.   II, iii, 10; DQ II, 42

Although all the attributes of God are equally
excellent, that of mercy has a better effect in our eye
and strikes with greater luster than justice.

II, iii, 10; DQ II, 42

The hypocrite who cloaks his knavery is less
dangerous to the commonwealth than he who
transgresses in the face of day.   II, ii, 7; DQ II, 24

There is nothing upon earth more productive of
honor and profit . . . than the service of the king.

II, ii, 7; DQ II, 24

As the king minds, the law binds.   II, i, 5; DQ II, 5

If you obey the commands of your lord, you may sit as
a guest at his board.   II, ii, 12; DQ II, 29

Two shepherdesses run into the unusual adventurers.

Adolphe Lalauze (1838–1906)

History

History is a sacred subject, because the soul of it is truth, and where truth is, there the divinity will reside.

II, i, 3; DQ II, 3

There is no human history that does not contain reverses of fortune.

II, i, 3; DQ II, 3

It requires great judgment and a ripe understanding to compose histories, or indeed any book whatsoever.

II, i, 3; DQ II, 3

All historians ought to be punctual, candid, and dispassionate, that neither interest, rancor, fear, nor affection may mislead them from the road of truth, whose mother is history.

I, ii, 1; DQ I, 9

Important and weighty historians . . . recount events so succinctly and superficially that the reader can scarce get a smack of them; while the most substantial circumstances are left, as it were, in the inkhorn, through carelessness, ignorance, and malice.

I, iii, 2; DQ I, 16

Hope

Hope [is] the food of desire.   I, ii, 5; DQ I, 14

It is better to be rich in hope than poor in possession.

II, i, 7; DQ II, 7

Righteous hope is better than unjust possession.

II, iv, 13; DQ II, 65

While there is life, there is hope.   II, iii, 7; DQ II, 39

Human Nature

We are all as God made us, and many of us much
worse.

II, i, 4; DQ II, 4

Scruples of conscience are very uncomfortable
companions.

II, i, 1; DQ II, 1

Though we love the treason, we abhor the traitor.

I, iv, 11; DQ I, 39

The wicked are always ungrateful.

I, iii, 9; DQ I, 23

Benefits conferred on base-minded people are like
drops of water thrown into the sea.

I, iii, 9; DQ I, 23

Once you receive an injury, you never forget it.

I, iii, 7; DQ I, 21

All the honors and disgraces of this life proceed from
flesh and blood.

I, iv, 6; DQ I, 33

Every creature procreates its own resemblance.

I, Prologue

The eyes of people always run slightly over the poor but make a halt to examine the rich.   II, i, 5; DQ II, 5

Pleasantry and wit . . . do not love to dwell in a reserved disposition.   II, ii, 13; DQ II, 30

Hunger

Hunger is the best sauce.   II, i, 5; DQ II, 5

Hearty fare lightens care.   II, i, 13; DQ II, 13

All ills are good when attended with food.
                                             II, iv, 3; DQ II, 55

Over the times and seasons of eating and drinking,
care seldom holds jurisdiction.   II, iv, 2; DQ II, 54

The toil and burthen [burden] of arms are not to be
borne without satisfying the cravings of the stomach.
                                             I, i, 2; DQ I, 2

Sure the man his lot may rue who has not broke his
fast by two.   II, iii, 1; DQ II, 33

Excess of wine will neither keep a secret nor perform
a promise.   II, iii, 11; DQ II, 43

A maid helps Sancho quench his thirst.

Gustave Doré (1832–1883)

Life as a Game;
Life as a Play

He is safe who has good cards to play.   II, iii, 4; DQ II, 36

One ought to lose the game by a card too much
rather than by a card too little.   II, iii, 1; DQ II, 33

Patience, and shuffle the cards [get on with life].

II, ii, 6; DQ II, 23

When the game [of chess] is over, [the pieces] are all
mixed, jumbled, and shaken together in a bag, like
mortals in the grave.   II, i, 12; DQ II, 12

Actors are ... ministers of mirth and pleasure; they
are favored, protected, assisted, and esteemed by
everybody.   II, i, 11; DQ II, 11

Comedy ... ought to be the mirror of life, the
exemplar of manners, and [the] picture of truth.

I, iv, 20; DQ I, 20

The Literary Arts

There is no book so bad but you may find something good in it.

II, i, 3; DQ II, 3

Fiction is always the better the nearer it resembles truth.

I, iv, 20; DQ I, 47

The perfection of writing consists in probability and imitation.

I, iv, 20; DQ I, 47

Writing is the interpreter of the mind.

II, i, 16; DQ II, 16

Sense is the foundation of good language, assisted by custom and use.

II, ii, 2; DQ II, 19

To write with elegance and wit is the province of great geniuses only.

II, i, 3; DQ II, 3

One of [the devil's] most effectual snares is to make a man believe that he has the capacity to write a book by which he shall obtain an equal share of money and reputation.

II, Prologue

He who publishes a book runs an immense risk because it is absolutely impossible to compose such a one as will please and entertain every reader.

II, i, 3; DQ II, 3

There are some who compose and cast off books as if they were tossing up a dish of pancakes.   II, i, 3; DQ II, 3

An author does not write with his gray hairs but according to the dictates of his understanding.

II, Prologue

An author had better be applauded by the few that are wise than laughed at by the many that are foolish.

I, iv, 21; DQ I, 48

The greater the reputation of the author is, the more severely are they scrutinized.   II, i, 3; DQ II, 3

[To] turn poet, they say, is an infectious and incurable distemper.   I, i, 6; DQ I, 6

A poet is born with his talent.   II, i, 16; DQ II, 16

Poetry ... is a kind of alchemy of such rare virtue that whoever knows the nature of her composition may change her into pure gold of inestimable value.

                                                    II, i, 16; DQ II, 16

The poet may relate or rehearse things, not as they were, but as they ought to have been; whereas a historian must transmit them, not as they ought to have been, but exactly as they were, without adding to or subtracting the least title from the truth.

                                                    II, i, 3; DQ II, 3

Art does not exceed nature but serves to polish and bring it into perfection.   II, i, 16; DQ II, 16

Books, books, books!

Gustave Doré (1832–1883)

Love and Marriage

Love . . . puts all things upon a level.   I, ii, 3; DQ I, 11

O jealousy! Love's tyrant lord.   I, ii, 5; DQ I, 14

True love must be undivided and unconstrained.
    I, ii, 5; DQ I, 14

That is the natural disposition of the sex [women] to
disdain those who adore them and love those by
whom they are abhorred.   I, iii, 6; DQ I, 20

He that loves thee well will often make thee cry.
    I, iii, 6; DQ I, 20

Love in young people is, for the most part, nothing
but appetite, whose only aim is pleasure.
    I, iii, 9; DQ I, 24

The two qualities which above all others inspire love
are beauty and reputation.   I, iii, 11; DQ I, 25

No man can command the first emotions of his
passion.   I, iv, 3; DQ I, 30

Love sometimes flies, sometimes walks, runs with one,
creeps with another, warms a third, burns a fourth,
wounding some, and slaying others. In one moment it
begins, performs, and concludes its career; lays siege in
the morning to a fortress, which is surrendered by
night, there being no force that can withstand its
power.   I, iv, 7; DQ I, 34

Opportunity is the best minister for executing the
designs of love.   I, iv, 7; DQ I, 34

Love, the powerful excuse of greater crimes.
                                            I, iv, 7; DQ I, 34

Love wears a pair of spectacles [that] make copper
look like gold, poverty appear to be riches, and specks
in the eyes to seem pearls.   II, ii, 2; DQ II, 19

Let every goose a gander choose.   II, ii, 2; DQ II, 19

Love and war are the same . . . it is lawful and
customary to use feints and stratagems against the
enemy, so likewise in amorous contests and
competitions all sorts of tricks and contrivances are
allowed in attaining the accomplishments of the
lover's desire, provided they do not tend to the
disparagement or dishonor of the beloved object.

II, ii, 4; DQ II, 21

The indignation of lovers usually vents itself in
maledictions.

II, iv, 15; DQ II, 67

The greatest enemy of love is hunger and necessity.

II, ii, 5; DQ II, 22

Nothing but divine force can subdue [love's] human
power.

I, iv, 7; DQ I, 37

Love and affection easily blind the eyes of the
understanding.

II, ii, 2; DQ II, 19

Don Quixote and Sancho Panza disrupt a wedding.

Francis Hayman (1708–1776)

A man ought not to visit and frequent the house of a friend after he is married in the same manner as he had practiced while he was single.   I, iv, 6; DQ I, 33

A man on whom heaven hath bestowed a beautiful wife should be cautious of the men he brings home to his house.   I, iv, 6; DQ I, 33

Marriage is a noose which, if the neck should happen to slip into it, becomes inexplicable as the Gordian knot and cannot be undone till cut asunder by the scythe of death.   II, ii, 2; DQ II, 19

We women are born to be obedient to our husbands, tho' they are no better than blocks.   II, i, 5; DQ II, 5

Madness and Foolishness

For men to execute signs [designs] which are clearly productive of more hurt than benefit is the province of madness and temerity.   I, iv, 6; DQ I, 33

Madness is always more accompanied and followed after than discretion.   II, i, 13; DQ II, 13

The world abounds much more with fools than people of sense.   I, iv, 21; DQ I, 48

The wisest person in the comedy is he that plays the fool.   II, i, 3; DQ II, 3

A fool knows more in his own house than a wise man in that of his neighbor's.   II, iii, 11; DQ II, 43

A wife's counsel is bad, but he that will not take it is mad.   II, i, 7; DQ II, 7

Tired of adventures, Sancho Panza returns to his family.

Francis Hayman (1708–1776)

Men and Women

A man must be a man and a woman a woman.

II, i, 7; DQ II, 7

Nothing is more commendable in beautiful women than modesty; and nothing more ridiculous than laughter proceeding from slight cause.

I, i, 2; DQ I, 2

Remember, my friend, that woman is an imperfect creature.

I, iv, 6; DQ I, 33

No jewel upon earth is comparable to a woman of virtue and honor.

I, iv, 6; DQ I, 33

A virtuous woman, like relics, ought to be adored at a distance.

I, iv, 6; DQ I, 33

Women have naturally more invention than man can boast of, either for a good or bad occasion.

I, iv, 7; DQ I, 34

Nothing sooner succeeds in overthrowing the
embattled towers of female vanity than vanity itself.

I, iv, 7; DQ I, 34

Between the Yes and No of a woman, I would not
venture to thrust the point of a pin.   II, ii, 2; DQ II, 19

By the modesty and reserve of young women . . .
amorous shafts are blunted and broken.   II, iv, 6; DQ II, 58

Nature

Don Quixote recruits Sancho Panza.

Gustave Doré (1832–1883)

The power called nature is like a potter who, if he can
make one beautiful vessel, can in like manner make
two.   II, ii, 13; DQ II, 30

The little birds of the field have God for their steward
and shield.   II, iii, 1; DQ II, 33

The viper deserves no blame for its sting, although it
be mortal, because it is the gift of nature.   I, ii, 5; DQ I, 14

Men have learned many things of importance from
beasts, such as . . . the use of vomits from dogs,
vigilance from the crane, foresight and frugality from
the ant, honesty from the elephant, and loyalty from
the horse.   II, i, 12; DQ II, 12

Melancholy was not made for beasts but for men; and
yet, if men encourage melancholy too much, they
became no better than beasts.   II, i, 11; DQ II, 11

Olla Podrida★:
A Miscellany

★ Literally, a meat and vegetable stew. Figuratively, a miscellany.

A mouth without grinders is like a mill without a millstone: a tooth is worth a treasure.   I, iii, 4; DQ I, 18

Never thrust your thumb between another man's grinders.   II, iii, 11; DQ II, 43

Once my tongue begins to itch, I cannot for my blood keep it within my teeth.   I, iv, 3; DQ I, 30

The proof of the pudding is in the eating of it.

I, iv, 10; DQ I, 37

He must be blind indeed that cannot see through the bottom of a sieve.   II, i, 1; DQ II, 1

What covers, discovers.   II, i, 5; DQ II, 5

He that buys and denies, his own purse belies.

I, iii, 11; DQ I, 25

The loyal Sancho inspects Don Quixote
for missing "grinders" after a fight.

Francis Hayman (1708–1776)

Everything ought to be esteemed in proportion to
what it costs.
I, iv, 11; DQ I, 38

A good claim is preferable to bad pay.
II, i, 7; DQ II, 7

There must be some worthy people even in hell.
II, iii, 2; DQ II, 34

From great ladies great benefits are expected.
II, ii, 15; DQ II, 32

There's as good bread baked here as in France.
II, iii, 1; DQ II, 33

The Pope's body takes up no more room than the
sexton's.
II, iii, 1; DQ II, 33

When we go to the pit we must lie snug and make it
fit.
II, iii, 1; DQ II, 33

A good drinker is found under a rusty cloak.

II, iii, 1; DQ II, 33

Make yourself honey and the flies will bite.

II, iii, 17; DQ II, 49

Sweet is the love of native land.   II, iv, 2; DQ II, 54

By night all cats are gray.   II, iii, 1; DQ II, 33

We knew not our happiness until we lost it.

II, iv, 2; DQ II, 54

Happy is he to whom heaven hath sent a morsel of bread, for which he is obliged to none but heaven itself.   II, iv, 6; DQ II, 58

Sudden joy kills as well as deadly sorrow.

II, iii, 20; DQ II, 52

Peace and Liberty

Sancho tricks Don Quixote into believing a country wench is his beloved Dulcinea, but the country wench is having none of it.

Francis Hayman (1708–1776)

Peace [is] the greatest good that mortals can enjoy.

I, iv, 10; DQ I, 37

Peace is a jewel without which there can be no
felicity, either in heaven or on earth!   I, iv, 10; DQ I, 37

Peace is the genuine aim of war, for arms and war are
the same.   I, iv, 10; DQ I, 37

God himself bestowed his blessing upon peace and
curse upon contention.   II, i, 14; DQ II, 14

Liberty is one of the most precious gifts which heaven
hath bestowed on man.   II, iv, 6; DQ II, 58

Captivity and restraint are the greatest evils that
human nature can endure.   II, iv, 6; DQ II, 58

There is no happiness on earth equal to that of liberty
regained.   I, iv, 12; DQ I, 39

Poverty

There are two families in the world ... the have-somethings and the have-nothings.   II, ii, 3; DQ II, 20

Nobility may be clouded by indigence but never altogether obscured.   II, Prologue

Virtue, shining by its own internal light, even through the inconveniencies and crannies of poverty, will recommend itself to the esteem of high and princely minds.   II, Prologue

A man who is poor ought to bless God for what he finds and not be diving to find truffles [the impossible] at the bottom of the sea.   II, ii, 3; DQ II, 20

He that is poor can enjoy nothing that is good but must endure necessity in all its forms, sometimes hunger, sometimes cold, sometimes nakedness, and, often, all three together.   I, iv, 10; DQ I, 37

The poor man is incapable of exerting the virtue of
liberality; let him possess it in never so eminent a
degree.   I, iv, 21; DQ I, 50

He that is getting aught is losing naught.   II, i, 7; DQ II, 7

Don Quixote attacks a windmill.

Gustave Doré (1832–1883)

Prosperity

There cannot be too much of a good thing. I, i, 6; DQ I, 6

Thou are worth just as much as thou hast, and hast just as much as thou art worth. II, ii, 3; DQ II, 20

If I lose nothing, as little I gain. I, iii, 11; DQ I, 25

There are two paths that lead to wealth and honor: one is that of learning, the other that of arms.

II, i, 6; DQ II, 6

While there are peas in the dove house, I shall never want [be without] pigeons. II, i, 7; DQ II, 7

Wealth is able to repair a number of flaws.

II, ii, 2; DQ II, 19

An ass loaded with gold will skip over a mountain.

II, iii, 3; DQ II, 35

An ass with golden trappings makes a better
appearance than a horse with a pack-saddle.

II, ii, 3; DQ II, 20

Upon a good foundation a good house may be raised,
and the very best bottom and best foundation of any
is wealth.

II, ii, 3; DQ II, 20

We are more apt to feel the pulse of property than of
wisdom.

II, ii, 3; DQ II, 20

The prodigal is more likely to become truly generous
than the miser.

II, i, 17; DQ II, 17

A dinner is easily got where there is plenty of meat for
the pot.

II, ii, 13; DQ II, 30

The house itself will tell if God loves its master well.

II, iii, 11; DQ II, 43

Don Quixote and Sancho attempt to leave an inn
without paying for their lodging.

Gustave Doré (1832–1883)

Prudence

Would it not be better to live in peace at home than to stray up and down the world in search of superfine bread, without considering that many a one goes out for wool and comes home quite shorn?   I, i, 7; DQ I, 7

To retreat is not to fly, nor is it prudent to tarry when the danger overbalances the hope: it is always the practice of wise people to reserve something for tomorrow without venturing all in one cast.

I, iii, 9; DQ I, 23

I prune my own vine and know nothing about thine.

I, iii, 11; DQ I, 25

Look before you leap.   II, i, 5; DQ II, 5

Better thieve than grieve. [Better to flee from danger.]

I, iii, 7; DQ I, 21

Forewarned and forearmed is half the day.

II, i, 17; DQ II, 17

One maxim of prudence is not to do ... by foul
means [that] which can be accomplished by fair.

I, iii, 8; DQ I, 22

It is surely better to avoid than await the battle.

II, iii, 16; DQ II, 48

The Quest

*Don Quixote on Rozinante and Sancho Panza on Dapple
begin their quest for adventure.*

Gustave Doré (1832–1883)

Let us live while we can, speak while we may, and at
present pursue our journey.   I, iii, 8; DQ I, 22

People sometimes go in quest of one thing and meet
with another.   I, iii, 2; DQ I, 16

It is one thing to undertake but another to finish.
                                          II, i, 15; DQ II, 15

There is no road so smooth but you'll meet with rubs
and hollows in it.   II, i, 13; DQ II, 13

They who go in search of adventures do not always
find them to their liking.   II, i, 13; DQ II, 13

The more I seek, the further I am from finding it.
                                          II, iii, 4; DQ II, 36.

He that seeketh danger perisheth therein.   I, iii, 6; DQ I, 20

Adventures and misadventures never begin with trifles.   I, iii, 6; DQ I, 20

[To go] in quest of a cat with three feet. [To look for trouble.]   I, iii, 8; DQ I, 22

Bare I was born and bare I remain, and if I lose nothing, as little I gain.   I, iii, 11; DQ I, 25

A prudent man who is resolved to undertake a long journey will, before he sets out, endeavor to find a safe, quiet, and agreeable fellow traveler.   II, ii, 2; DQ II, 19

Delay breeds danger.   II, iii, 9; DQ II, 41

Sleep

While we sleep, great and small, rich and poor, are all
equal.   II, iii, 11; DQ II, 43

Sleep is a remedy for those miseries which we feel
when awake.   II, iv, 18; DQ II, 70

Sleep resembles death inasmuch as between a dead
corpse and a sleeping man there is no apparent
difference.   II, iv, 16; DQ II, 68

Praise be to him who invented sleep, which is the
mantle that shrouds all human thoughts, the food that
dispels hunger, the drink that quenches thirst, the fire
that warms the cold, the cool breeze that moderates
heat; in a word, the general coin that purchases every
commodity; the weight and balance that makes the
shepherd even with his sovereign and the simple with
the sage.   II, iv, 16; DQ II, 68

Time

There is nothing that time, the discoverer of all things, will not bring to light, even though it be hidden in the bowels of the earth.   II, ii, 8; DQ II, 25

The malignity of time . . . wastes and devours all things.   I, ii, 1; DQ I, 9

There is no remembrance that time does not efface nor pain that death does not remove.   I, iii, 1; DQ I, 15

What greater misfortune can there be than that which nothing but time can remove or death put a stop to?
                                                   I, iii, 1; DQ I, 15

Make the best of a bad bargain and leave the rest to time, who is [the] best physician for [these and other] greater calamities.   II, i, 11; DQ II, 11

Time is so light and nimble that no rub can retard his career.   II, iii, 14; DQ II, 46

Time turns round on an incessant wheel.   II, iv, 1; DQ II, 53

There is still sunshine on the wall. [It is not too late.]

II, i, 3; DQ II, 3

Touché:
Insults and Ridicule

Dorotea asks Don Quixote to slay a giant enchanter.

Gustave Doré (1832–1883)

Honey was not made for the mouth of an ass.

I, iv, 25; DQ I, 52

You excommunicated rascal! I, iv, 3; DQ I, 30

You groveling beggarly villain ... viperish scoffer!

I, iv, 3; DQ I, 30

Thou foul-mouthed, unmannerly, insolent, and malicious slanderer! I, iv, 19; DQ I, 46

Get out of my sight, monster of nature, depository of flies, cupboard of deceit, granary of knavery, inventor of mischief, publisher of folly, and foe to that respect that is due royalty! I, iv, 19; DQ I, 46

Swag-bellied lurcher! II, i, 2; DQ II, 2

Housekeeper of Satan! Cursed cormorant, gorbellied glutton, bag of mischief, and bundle of malice!

II, i, 2; DQ II, 2

You beast and yoke-fellow for Barabbas!   II, i, 5; DQ II, 5

Animal with half an eye!   II, i, 5; DQ II, 5

You ignorant beast . . . as thou hast neither capacity to understand my discourse nor prudence to make sure of good fortune.   II, i, 5; DQ II, 5

O miserable, hard-hearted animal!   II, iii, 3; DQ II, 35

Thou soul of a garret mouse!   II, ii, 12; DQ II, 29

[You] garlic-eating rascal!   II, ii, 14; DQ II, 31

Thou modern buffoon and ancient blockhead!
    II, ii, 14; DQ II, 31

Thou soul of a pitcher, heart of cork, and bowels of flinty pebbles!   II, iii, 3; DQ II, 35

Chastise, chastise, obdurate beast, that brawny beef of thine.   II, iii, 3; DQ II, 35

You knavish son of a whore and painter for the devil himself!   II, iii, 15; DQ II, 47

What a heart of marble, bowels of brass, and soul of plaster!   II, iv, 6; DQ II, 58

Miscreant! ... is it possible there should be a person upon earth who would not say thou art stark mad and that thy soul is lined and bordered with fillets of malice and knavery?   II, iv, 6; DQ II, 58

Oh ill-digested bread!   II, iv, 16; DQ II, 68

[You] stone of a date!   II, iv, 18; DQ II, 70

Our heroes encounter angry bulls.

Gustave Doré (1832–1883)

Truth

Truth may bend, but it will never break, and always surmounts falsehood as oil floats above water.

II, i, 10; DQ II, 10

A man ought to examine things with more senses than one before he can be assured of the truth.

II, i, 11; DQ II, 11

There is not so much proof and counterproof required to bring the truth to light. II, ii, 9; DQ II, 26

God knows the truth, and there let it lie. I, iv, 20; DQ I, 47

The naked truth will always swim above falsehood like oil above water. II, iii, 18; DQ II, 50

Vice

Evil tongues will not refrain from God himself.

I, iii, 11; DQ I, 25

He that hath good in his view, yet will not evil
eschew, his folly deserveth to rue.
I, iv, 4; DQ I, 31

One of the sins that gives the greatest offense to God
is ingratitude.
I, iii, 8; DQ I, 22

Hell is crowded with the ungrateful.
II, iv, 6; DQ II, 58

Greediness bursts the bag.
I, iii, 6; DQ I, 20

What's honestly earn'd may be easily lost, but ill-got
wealth is ever at the owner's cost.
II, iv, 2; DQ II, 54

From the children of envy no thriving person is
secure.
II, i, 5; DQ II, 5

The adventurers return to their village.

Gustave Doré (1832–1883)

Envy produces nothing in the heart that harbors it but rage, rancor, and disgust.

II, i, 8; DQ II, 8

Just are virtue's fears where envy domineers.

I, iv, 20; DQ I, 47

We must, in slaying giants, extirpate pride; get the better of envy by benevolence and virtue; resist anger with patience and forbearance; conquer gluttony and sloth by temperance and watchfulness; luxury and lewdness by our fidelity to those whom we constitute the mistresses of our inclination; and idleness by traveling through all parts of the world in quest of opportunities to evince ourselves not only Christians but, moreover, renowned knights.

II, i, 8; DQ II, 8

Every new fault deserves a new penance.

I, iv, 3; DQ I, 30

Ingratitude is the daughter of pride.

II, iii, 19; DQ II, 51

Virtue

True nobility consists in virtue.   I, iv, 9; DQ I, 36

Virtue is so powerful that of herself she will ... come off conqueror in every severe trial and shine refulgent in the world as the sun shines in the heavens.

I, iv, 20; DQ I, 47

The path of virtue is very straight while the road of vice is broad and spacious.   II, i, 6; DQ II, 6

Virtue is always more persecuted by the wicked than beloved by the righteous.   I, iv, 20; DQ I, 47

Whenever virtue shines [to] an eminent degree, she always meets with persecution.   II, i, 2; DQ II, 2

What is learning without virtue? No better than pearls on a dung hill.   II, i, 16; DQ II, 16

It is the duty of honest men to be thankful for benefits received.   I, iii, 8; DQ I, 22

Gratitude which is restrained to goodwill alone is like
faith without works.   I, iv, 23; DQ I, 50

Let it still be thy view all mischief to eschew.

II, iv, 4; DQ II, 56

The arduous life of a knight and his squire.

Gustave Doré (1832–1883)

Wisdom and Learning

It requires a good brain to know when to give and
[when to] retain.   II, iii, 11; DQ II, 43

The fear of God is the beginning of wisdom.
                                                     II, ii, 3; DQ II, 20

The beginning of health is knowledge of the disease.
                                                     II, iv, 8; DQ II, 60

If the servant is so wise, what must the master be?
                                                     II, iv, 14; DQ II, 66

If the master be as wise as the man . . . we have
brought our pigs to a fine market.   II, ii, 14; DQ II, 31

The man in wisdom must be old, who knows in
giving where to hold.   II, iv, 6; DQ II, 58

I am an old dog and will not be coaxed with a crust.
                                                     II, iii, 1; DQ II, 33

He who does not rise with the sun cannot enjoy the day.
II, iii, 11; DQ II, 43

Let us [not look] for this year's birds in last year's nests.
II, iv, 21; DQ II, 74

All proverbs ... are true ... because they are short sentences dictated by long and sage experience.
I, iv, 12; DQ I, 39

For a man to be totally devoid of letters, or left-handed, argues either that he was descended from the lowest and meanest of people or that he was so wicked and stubborn that good example and judicious precepts have had no effect upon his mind or understanding.
II, iii, 11; DQ II, 43

A rich man's folly is wisdom in the world's eye.
II, iii, 11; DQ II, 43

No man was ever a scholar at his birth.
II, iii, 1; DQ II, 33

Don Quixote's Epitaph

Here lies a cavalier of fame,
    Whose dauntless courage soar'd so high,
That death, which can the boldest tame,
    He scorned to flatter or to fly.
A constant bugbear to the bad,
    His might the world in arms defied,
And in his life though counted mad,
    He in his perfect senses died.

II, iv, 22; DQ II, 74

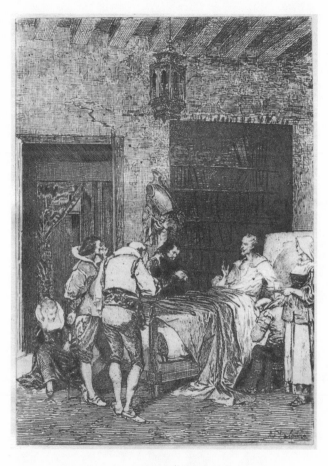

*Don Quixote regains his senses and says farewell
to his friends and family.*

Adolphe Lalauze (1838–1906)

A Note on the Themes

The Wit and Wisdom of Don Quixote de la Mancha is grouped thematically, and many of these themes—adversity, friendship, hunger, love, sleep—need no explanatory note. But some themes, either because of their special place in the novel or because of their meaning within Renaissance literature, merit some comment.

We began with **Our Players**, short quotes from the text describing the major players in the novel. If you have already read the Introduction, then you know about Don Quixote and Sancho Panza. In Book One, Don Quixote is dubbed the Knight of the Rueful Countenance by Sancho, who describes him as "the most dismal figure [he had] ever seen ... occasioned either by fatigue ... or by the want of ... teeth" (I, iii, 5; DQ I, 19). In Book Two, Don Quixote dubs himself as Knight of the Lions after he "defeats" a circus lion, who in reality would rather nap in his cage (II, i, 17; DQ II, 17). Dulcinea del Toboso is the woman of Don Quixote's heart—except that she doesn't strictly exist. Don Quixote, in desiring a lady to whom to devote his adventures, imagines that a local country wench, Aldonza, is in fact a beautiful, noble lady. Sancho is perplexed and vexed by Quixote's devotion to Dulcinea and at one point tricks our hero into believing a homely traveling peasant girl is Dulcinea under enchantment. Several of our descriptions concern both the beautiful and the homely versions of Dulcinea/Aldonza.

Since Don Quixote sets off to be a knight-errant, there are many chapters devoted to the martial life he craves: **Arms and the Man**; **Courage**; **Fame, Honor, and Reputation**; and **The Quest**. Cervantes, of course an old soldier himself, has much to say through Don Quixote and others about how the man of arms should comport himself and about the rigors of military life. Cervantes balances these observations with views on the literary life and the challenges of being a man of letters. **The Literary Arts** and **Life as a Game; Life as a Play** touch on themes of art and life and are fairly representational of Renaissance conceits.

Fortune in Cervantes's time referred to destiny, to fate, and in literature and real life was an important concept. Fortune was often symbolized as a turning wheel and characterized as an uncontrollable, implacable force but often countered by the notion of divine providence.

In the **Men and Women** chapter, there is a preponderance of quotations about women, not all complimentary and most condescending to a modern ear. It almost goes without saying that these sayings reflect a very different time, when a woman's place in the world was defined by her status as a chaste maiden, an obedient wife, or an honorable widow. Even so, *Don Quixote de la Mancha* features some delightfully outspoken ladies, one of whom is Sancho's wife, Teresa, who is prepared to call her husband a "blockhead." Another example is Marcela, who defends her freedom by refusing to marry a man simply because she is expected to do so.

Olla Podrida is a "stew" of proverbs or witty sayings that is difficult to classify under one category. The quotations about the importance of teeth truly reflect a time when teeth were valuable commodities and appropriate dental care was nonexistent! Observations on sleep, blindness, insight, self-deception, trickery, expectation, ignorance, and time reflect the wisdom of everyday experience.

Virtue and **Vice** were very important concepts in the seventeenth century. Many of the quotations in the vice section concern the seven deadly sins: lust, greed, sloth, envy, anger, pride, and gluttony. The seven virtues—faith, hope, charity, temperance, fortitude, prudence, and justice—are also found in the categories of **Governance and Justice**, **Human Nature**, and **Men and Women**.